The
Land
o'
Burns

A GUIDE TO
THE BURNS COUNTRY

JAMES MACKAY

The Burns Country, covering the former counties of Ayrshire, Dumfriesshire, Kirkcudbrightshire and Wigtownshire.

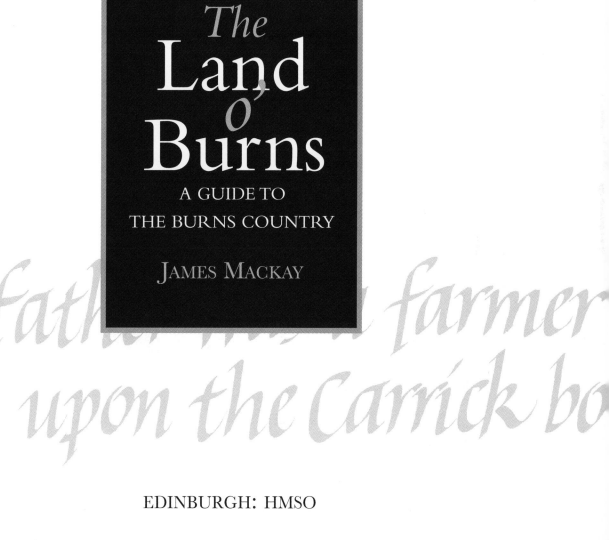

The Land o' Burns

A GUIDE TO
THE BURNS COUNTRY

JAMES MACKAY

My father was a farmer upon the Carrick bo

EDINBURGH: HMSO

© James Mackay 1996
First published 1996

Designed by Derek Munn, HMSO Graphic Design (2734)
Illustrations by Steve Earl

British Library Cataloguing in Publication Data
A catalogue record for this book is available from the British Library

Every care has been taken to make the information as accurate as possible in this book, but the author and publishers can accept no responsibility for errors however caused.
The opening times are believed to be correct at the time of going to press, but may be subject to seasonal and time variation particularly during the Burns bicentenary year celebrations in 1996.
For accurate information, contact the appropriate venues.

Cover illustration (front and inside) of Robert Burns by Alexander Nasmyth, reproduced by kind permission of The Scottish National Portrait Gallery

ISBN 0 11 495766 5

CONTENTS

INTRODUCTION AND ACKNOWLEDGEMENTS

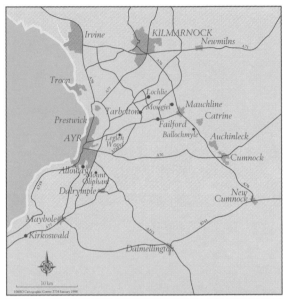

The Land o' Burns, or the Burns Country, is that part of Ayrshire roughly comprising the ancient baileries of Cunninghame, Kyle and north Carrick where the poet spent the first twenty-nine years of his life, together with much of present-day Dumfries and Galloway where he settled in 1788 and lived until his untimely death eight years later. This book is designed for those who wish to follow the course of his life and visit the places associated with him.

Broadly speaking, the Land o' Burns cuts a swathe through the southwest of Scotland; an arc that begins with north Carrick, taking in his birthplace, Alloway, as well as Maybole (home of his maternal ancestors) and Kirkoswald (where he studied mathematics), then via Ayr to Tarbolton and Mauchline (where he farmed), Irvine (where he learned the trade of flax-dressing) and Kilmarnock (where his *Poems* were first published). The A76 trunk road takes us through the beautiful Doon Valley and Nithsdale, past New Cumnock and Sanquhar where he often lodged overnight while travelling between his old home at Mossgiel and his new farm at Ellisland, to Dumfries where he resided in the last five years of his life. He made excursions to Wanlockhead, Castle Douglas and Newton Stewart, while his Excise duties took him to Lochmaben and Ecclefechan, Penpont and Moniaive; but though these towns have their associations with Burns they have not left us any tangible memorial of the poet and for that reason they have been excluded.

I have concentrated on the places where Robert Burns lived, the farms where he worked, and the towns and villages which boast a museum or a memorial or some other place of interest which has an obvious link with the poet. In a brief survey of this nature it is impossible to enumerate all the places associated with the friends of Burns, or those which received a mention in his poetry or his voluminous correspondence. Readers seeking such information, however, should consult *The Ayrshire Book of Burns-Lore* by Andrew M. Boyle and *Burns-Lore of Dumfries and Galloway* by myself (both by Alloway Publishing) which provide an alphabetical listing of all places, past and present, connected directly or indirectly with Burns and his writings. For fuller details of the various statues, plaques and memorials, my book *Burnsiana* (Alloway Publishing) should be consulted.

I am grateful to Gordon Borthwick of the National Trust for Scotland for kindly supplying the pictures of the Tarbolton Bachelors' Club and Souter Johnie's Cottage at Kirkoswald. I was unable to take pictures of these two locations as they were the subject of major renovation during 1995. The rest of the pictures were supplied by a combination of myself and the HMSO photographers, Stephen Kearney and Paul Watt. The illustrations were done by Steve Earl.

JAMES MACKAY

(opposite) Maps of the areas around Ayr, Kilmarnock and Dumfries.

My father was
upon the C

BURNS COTTAGE
Robert Burns the Ayrshire poet
was born in this cottage
on the 25th Jan A.D 1759
and died 21st July A.D 1796 age 37½ years

1
BURNS'S EARLY LIFE, 1759-84

Robert Burns, the Scottish poet and Bard of All Humanity, was born on 25 January 1759, the eldest of seven children (four sons and three daughters) born to William Burnes and his wife Agnes Brown. William had left Kincardineshire in 1748, worked for a time as a landscape gardener in Edinburgh, then moved to Ayrshire where he was employed on the Fairlie and Doonholm estates. In 1757 he married Agnes Brown of Craigenton, Maybole and leased seven and a half acres of ground from his employer, Provost Fergusson of Doonholm, with the idea of establishing a market garden. On a portion of this land he built, with his own hands, a long, single-storey cottage and byre. The 'auld cley biggin' known as **Burns Cottage**, with its whitewashed walls and thatched roof, survives to this day and is located in **Alloway**, originally a small village on the banks of the River Doon two miles (3.2 km) south of Ayr but nowadays an affluent suburb of that town. The cottage fronts onto the present B7024 Ayr-Maybole road, although prior to 1815 the road ran to the west of the cottage.

About 4 February 1759 a severe storm struck Ayrshire and badly damaged the cottage; Agnes and her infant son were evacuated to a neighbouring farmhouse until the roof and gable-end could be repaired. In due course three other children were born in this cottage: Gilbert (28 September 1760), Agnes (30 September 1762) and Annabella (14 November 1764). The cottage continued to be the Burnes home until 1766, but long before that time William had abandoned his plans of market-

Burns Cottage, Alloway.

1

gardening and had decided to lease a farm. For fifteen years (1766-81) William leased his cottage and land to a series of tenants, but eventually sold it to the Incorporation of Shoemakers in Ayr who, in turn, let it as an alehouse. In this role, enhanced by the celebrity of the poet, it continued till 1881 when it was purchased for £4000 by the Trustees of the Burns Monument and eventually restored. It is interesting to note that, five years after the poet's death, nine of his friends gathered at the cottage to hold a commemorative dinner in July 1801, and repeated the custom thereafter each January on his birthday, thus establishing the practice of Burns Suppers. The restoration of the cottage took twenty years, but it was inaugurated in 1901 and is now open daily from 9am till 7pm.

Numerous relics of the poet, together with a large library and one of the finest collections of Burns manuscripts now extant, have been assembled over the years and are now housed in the adjoining **Birthplace Museum**, open all year round with seasonal variations (tel: 01292 441215).

Some 300 metres south of Burns Cottage, on the west side of the road, lies the ruined **Kirk Alloway**, erected about 1516 but disused by 1691, briefly restored in 1740-52 and falling into ruin by the 1760s. It would provide the scene for the witches' dance in Burns's mock epic 'Tam o' Shanter'. To the kirkyard, in February 1764, were brought the mortal remains of William Burnes, whose tombstone (much pillaged by souvenir hunters and twice restored) is prominent near the entrance.

Across the road stands the **Tam o' Shanter Experience** visitor centre, formerly the Land o' Burns Centre which opened in June 1977, but which was recently enlarged and refurbished. It boasts an excellent souvenir shop, audio-visual centre, static displays of farming implements, a cafeteria and paved car-park, and is open all year round with seasonal variations (tel: 01292 443700).

To the south is the **National Burns Monument** set in

(above) Tombstone of William Burnes.
(below) Burns Monument, Alloway.

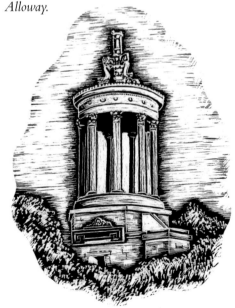

Alloway Kirk.

Burns Monument, Alloway.

attractive gardens on the north bank of the River Doon. The idea of a memorial to Burns was first mooted at Ayr on 24 March 1814 by Alexander Boswell of Auchinleck and the Revd Hamilton Paul (who had organised the commemorative dinner at the cottage in 1801). They eventually raised £3300 which paid for the monument designed by Thomas Hamilton of Edinburgh in the Grecian style. The monument, inaugurated in 1823, consists of a three-sided rustic basement supporting a circular Corinthian peristyle surmounted by a cupola. Each side faces one of the historic divisions of Ayrshire—Carrick, Cunninghame and Kyle. A circular chamber in the basement was designed to house relics of the poet, while the superstructure has nine columns representing the muses. The monument was the focal point for the great festival of 1844 celebrating the reunion of the poet's three surviving sons. The gardens contain life-sized stone figures of Tam o' Shanter, Souter Johnie, the landlord and his wife, from Burns's comic masterpiece, carved by James Thom. The monument and gardens are open daily from April till October (tel: 01292 441215).

Across the lane is the **Burns Monument Hotel** whose own beautifully landscaped gardens run down to the riverbank and provide the best view of the old **Brig o' Doon**. Situated 200 metres upstream from the present main road, it is open to pedestrian traffic only. The high-backed single-arched bridge is believed to date from the thirteenth century and is of interest chiefly as the location of the climax of 'Tam o' Shanter' when the witch Nanie caught Tam's mare Meg by the tail 'on the keystane o' the brig'.

Those who wish to trace Tam o' Shanter's erratic journey from Ayr to Shanter farm have the choice of two routes south from the town, along the A719 Ayr-Dunure road or, more probably, the B7024 Ayr-Maybole road via Alloway, across the Slaphouse Burn in Belleisle Park at the ford 'whare in the snaw the chapman smoor'd' [smothered or drowned]. Passing to the west of Burns Cottage, Tam would have ridden 'thro the whins and by the cairn, whare hunters fand the murder'd bairn'. The ancient cairn was moved from its original site in 1964 during redevelopment and a burial kist found underneath. In 1965 a commemorative cairn was erected between houses 5 and 7 on **Cairn Crescent** and embellished with a bronze plaque. Benches flanking it have been presented by the Burns clubs of Sydney, Australia and Ndola, Zambia. On the steep north bank of the river, by the north end of the disused railway

(left) Tam pursued by Nanie, on the Brig o' Doon.

Brig o' Doon, Alloway.

bridge which formerly crossed the river, is **St Mungo's Well**, alluded to in the poem but unmarked and approachable only by a scramble down the embankment of the disused line, through the tunnel under the main road and visible over the west parapet.

Alloway Village Hall, across the road from Burns Cottage, contains two plaster lunettes with friezes depicting scenes from 'The Jolly Beggars', as well as a bronze maquette of the statue, by James Pittendreigh MacGillivray, which stands on Irvine Town Moor (see p. 14). To the north of Alloway stands **Belleisle House**, now a hotel but formerly the country seat of the Glentanar family who commissioned Italian craftsmen to carve the figures, bas-reliefs and friezes that adorn the main hallway. In particular, the fireplace which stands opposite the reception desk shows Tam pursued by Nanie as the chief motif, surmounted by a group showing Burns at the plough with his birthplace in the background. Panels at the sides feature scenes from 'Death and Dr Hornbook', 'Tam o' Shanter' and 'The Jolly Beggars' while the Twa Dogs stand guard on the fireside benches. Above the main doorway are further wood panels illustrating 'John Anderson My Jo'.

The entire parish of **Ayr** had a population of only 2964 in 1775, so the market town itself must have been quite a small place. Nevertheless, it was the focal point of the Burnes family, where they traded their produce on market days, where they worshipped each Sabbath and where resided John Murdoch who gave Robert and Gilbert Burns the little formal education they received. The town figures prominently in many of the poet's works, most notably in 'Tam o' Shanter' where it was immortalised in the couplet:

Auld Ayr, wham ne'er a toun surpasses
For honest men and bonie lasses

as well as in the long poem 'The Brigs o' Ayr' recording an imaginary conversation between the **Auld** and **New Brigs**. Burns was prophetic when he had the Auld Brig tell the upstart built in 1786: 'I'll be a brig when ye're a shapeless cairn'. In fact, the New Brig collapsed in 1877 and only the uprights can be seen to this day. The Auld Brig, erected about 1232, is still used by pedestrians and was restored in 1910. The present road bridge stands close to the site of the New Brig, with the **Burns Tavern** on the north side.

On the east side of the High Street stands the **Tam o' Shanter Inn**, a fine example of an early eighteenth-century town house, complete with bottle-glass windows and thatch. Apart from being contemporary with Burns, however, it has no actual connection with either the poet or his famous creation, but in the hands of the Shearer family it was developed as a museum of Burnsiana which is well worth a visit. Apart from the obligatory painted, cast-metal heads of Tam and Johnie mounted on the wall there is a mural above the doorway of Tam about to mount his grey mare Meg. On the pavement outside is a stone in which is incised six lines of the poem. The small museum contains a library and a vast range of relics, souvenirs and ephemera.

Through the exertions of the Ayr Burns Club a fund was raised and the London sculptor George Lawson commissioned to produce the bronze statue of the poet which was unveiled on 8 July 1891 in a small circular park known to this day as **Burns Statue** Square. The statue has a set of four bronze bas-reliefs set into the sides of the pedestal. Lawson himself sculpted the panels showing Tam o' Shanter and Cutty Sark at the keystane o' the brig, and a scene from 'The Cotter's Saturday Night'. David McGill of Ayrshire sculpted the panel, presented by the Freemasons of Scotland, showing a racy scene from 'The Jolly Beggars', while the fourth, or American, panel was the gift of 25 citizens of the United States and was sculpted by George Bissell of Poughkeepsie, New York, showing the tender parting of Burns

(top) Burns Tavern, Ayr.
(middle) Tam o' Shanter Inn, Ayr.
(bottom) Interior of the Tam o' Shanter Inn, Ayr.

Burns and Highland Mary bas-relief on the Burns Statue, Ayr.

and Highland Mary. Casts of the Lawson statue were subsequently erected in Melbourne, Vancouver, Montreal and Winnipeg, while half-sized maquettes may be found in Ayr Old Church, Belfast Art Gallery and the Sorbonne, Paris. Incidentally, the statue even gives its name to the Burns Statue post office opened on the north side of the square in 1940, whose postmarks are much sought after by philatelists.

About 1765 Provost William Fergusson purchased the farm of **Mount Oliphant**, about two miles (3.2 km) south-east of Alloway. This small farm of about 90 acres on rising ground is half a mile (less than 1 km) south of the Corton road and a similar distance east of the present A77. Though the farm was in a rundown condition, William Burnes agreed to lease it for a rental of £40 a year, to be raised to £45 after six years. The twelve-year lease ran from Martinmas (11 November) 1765 till Martinmas 1777, though it contained a clause giving the tenant the option of removing at the end of six years. The Burnes

Mount Oliphant (rear view).

family did not actually move to this steading until Whitsun 1766. Gilbert Burns later described the farm as having 'almost the very poorest soil I know of in a state of cultivation'—a sweeping understatement for the ruinous bargain this proved to be. With the move to Mount Oliphant, the formal education of the Burnes boys under John Murdoch came to an end and henceforth the brothers, now aged seven and almost six, were set to work as farm labourers. Fortunately Murdoch had motivated them well, and they would profit by self-education which young Robert pursued voraciously. A list of the books which he read during this period is staggering in its range and complexity. The last three children of William and Agnes were born at Mount Oliphant: William (1767-90), John (1769-85) and Isabella (1771-1858).

After the light, sandy soil of Alloway, William Burnes had to wrestle with the mossy and moorish, the stony and inadequately drained land of this hill farm. The farmhouse itself was a poor, rough little place—a sketch of it in 1827 shows that no improvements had been wrought in the half century since William Burnes relinquished his tenancy. In later years, however, it would be largely rebuilt and refurbished, although the general ground-plan, on three sides of a courtyard, has been retained to this day. It is still a working farm, mainly given to the pasturage of dairy cattle and sheep, and from its exposed, windswept slopes it commands a fine view of Arran and the Firth of Clyde.

Appalled by the state of their handwriting, William Burnes sent his eldest sons back to school in 1772, Robert and Gilbert taking turns, week about, to attend the village school in the nearby village of **Dalrymple**. The school no longer exists but its site is occupied by the White Horse Hotel. One of the books which made a great impression on Robert at this period was an edition of Blind Harry's epic tale of Sir William Wallace, inspiring the lad to make a pilgrimage one Sunday from Mount Oliphant to **Leglen Wood** which had been one of the hero's hiding places.

Souter Johnie's Cottage, Kirkoswald.

In November 1786 Burns, writing to Wallace's kinswoman, Mrs Dunlop of Dunlop, described this boyhood jaunt. In 1929 the Burns Federation erected a cairn in the wood, just off the road from Auchencruive to Belston, linking the names of Wallace and Burns.

The Mount Oliphant period is also notable for kindling in Robert the desire to rhyme and compose songs. At harvest-time in 1774 he was paired with a girl a year younger and for her wrote the lyrics of 'Handsome Nell'. The heroine was originally named as Helen Blair, but from 1851 till 1992 she was identified (by Robert Chambers) as Helen Kilpatrick. As this girl was only weeks younger than Burns and her subsequent life does not fit the known facts, it seems that Helen Blair (identified in 1828) was indeed the correct person.

Robert's formal education was completed, in the summer of 1775, by several weeks spent at **Kirkoswald**, a village near the south Ayrshire coast, on the A77 road between Maybole and Girvan. This had been the home of the poet's maternal ancestors whose remains are interred in the kirkyard, alongside those of such worthies as Douglas Graham and Helen McTaggart, the originals of Tam and Kate, John Davidson (Souter Johnie) and Jean Kennedy (Kirkton Jean) immortalised in 'Tam o' Shanter'. The cottage in which John Davidson lived with his wife Ann Gillespie has been preserved by The National Trust for Scotland as **Souter Johnie's Cottage**, with life-sized stone figures of Tam, Johnie, the innkeeper and his wife by James Thom in the restored alehouse in the cottage garden. The thatched cottage contains Burns relics and the souter's workshop, and is open to the public from Good Friday to Easter Monday (1.30 - 5.30pm) 1st May to the end of September (1.30pm - 5.30pm) and from 1 to 31 October Saturdays and Sundays only (1.30 to 5.30pm), or by appointment with the curator at other times (tel: 01655 760603, cottage, or 01655 760671, home).

Robert lodged with Robert Niven, the farmer and miller of

Lochlie Farm, showing windswept, boggy terrain.

Ballochneil on the A77 two miles (3.2 km) south of the village. Niven was the father-in-law of Samuel Brown, the poet's uncle on his mother's side. Every day Robert trudged into Kirkoswald to study mensuration, trigonometry and calculus under Hugh Rodger (1726-1801), the village dominie and a celebrated mathematician. It was at Kirkoswald, a notorious smuggling haunt, that Robert 'learned to look unconcernedly on a large tavern-bill' and also, for the first time, fell madly in love—an episode which he described vividly in his Autobiographical Letter using mathematical metaphors. The 'charming Fillette' who set him off 'in a tangent from the sphere' of his studies was Margaret 'Peggy' Thomson. His first love made a lasting impression, for she was one of the few recipients of a signed copy of the Kilmarnock *Poems* in 1786, with a poignant eight-line inscription beginning:

> *Once fondly lov'd, and still remember'd dear,*
> *Sweet early object of my youthful vows,*

and before preparing for his proposed voyage to Jamaica he paid her one last visit, though she was by that time married.

North of Kirkoswald, and ten miles (16 km) south of Ayr on the A77 road, lies the town of **Maybole**, where Robert's mother Agnes Brown resided for thirteen years (1744-57). Agnes met William Burnes at the Maybole Fair in the summer of 1756, and local tradition maintains that the site of the booth at the fairground where they met is now occupied by the shop at 15 High Street which has a bust of Robert Burns mounted on the apex of the gable. William Niven (1761-1844), kinsman of John Niven of Ballochneil, was a fellow-pupil at Rodger's school and afterwards corresponded with the poet, whose letters to him are the earliest now extant. William became a prosperous businessman and served on Maybole's Town Council before becoming Depute Lieutenant for Ayrshire. Burns lodged at the King's Arms at 70 High Street (later destroyed by fire) in 1788

while travelling round the county collecting subscriptions to his *Poems*.

Dr Fergusson died in 1776 and his estate was divided among his four daughters. A factor administered the estate and chased up the bad debts, including the arrears of rent due by William Burnes. In the end the executors settled the matter by taking a mortgage on the Alloway smallholding which enabled Burnes to extricate himself from Mount Oliphant when the lease expired. He then took the farm of **Lochlie**, of 130 acres at 20 shillings an acre, in the parish of Tarbolton. This farm, nowadays spelled Lochlea, lies about two and a half miles (4 km) northeast of the village of Tarbolton in the parish of that name, and just over three miles (4.8 km) northwest of the town of Mauchline. The present farmhouse is considerably larger than the one occupied by the Burnes family and is situated on the road between Largie Toll and Craigie, a mile and a half (2.4 km) south of the A719 Ayr-Galston road. Much farther inland than Mount Oliphant, the farm is about 400 feet (130m) above sea-level and even more desolate than their previous abode, although nowadays a thick belt of woodland gives it shelter from the prevailing winds, and the ditches and hedgerows of later generations have broken up what must have been a featureless landscape in the eighteenth century.

The present house, a two-storey structure, was substantially rebuilt in the nineteenth century and the range of byres and barns is much more extensive than it was in the 1770s. A bronze plaque on the wall of one of the outbuildings is believed to mark the precise site of the steading of Burns's time. The farmhouse nestled in a depression, near the marsh-ringed loch which gave the farm its name. The loch was drained in the 1840s but in 1777 it was still very much in evidence and made field drainage exceedingly difficult. Even today the soil is heavy with a tendency to retain surface water. Without adequate capital, far less modern techniques of field drainage and soil improvement available to him, it is small wonder that William Burnes got into debt with his new landlord, David McClure. The matter went to litigation in 1782-84 and though William Burnes eventually won his case in the High Court of Edinburgh it broke him and he died in February 1784. By that time his eldest sons had taken steps to secure the lease of Mossgiel as security for the family.

To the Lochlie period belong some of the poet's happiest years, notwithstanding the drudgery and hardships. His skill as a poet developed and he entered into social life, becoming, with Gilbert, a founder member of the **Tarbolton Bachelors' Club** which met in John Richard's alehouse in the Sandgate for the first time on 11 November 1780. In 1938 the building was purchased by The National Trust for Scotland and is now open as a museum of Burns relics and period furnishings, from Good Friday to the end of September daily (1.30-5.30pm) and 1 to 22 October and weekends (1.30-5.30pm) or at other times by appointment with the curator (tel: 01292 541940).

It was also in this building, in the summer of 1781, that Burns was initiated into Freemasonry at Lodge St David, although today the masonic lodge is located in **Montgomerie Street**, with a commemorative plaque above the doorway. The **Plough Inn** at the lower end of this street has an unusual polychrome bust of the poet mounted on the external wall. South of the B744 Tarbolton-Galston road on the eastern outskirts of the village is **Tarbolton Mill**, referred to by Burns in 'Death and Doctor Hornbook' as Willie's Mill, after his friend William Muir who was then the miller. It was here, according to brother Gilbert, that Burns was in the habit of meeting 'Montgomerie's Peggy' (Margaret Campbell, otherwise known to posterity as 'Highland Mary') when she was the byrewoman at Coilsfield House.

In the summer of 1781 Burns had an unhappy affair with Elizabeth Gebbie, the housekeeper at Carnell House who later married Hugh Brown, a stocking-maker of Newmilns. Feeling

(above) Tarbolton Bachelors' Club.
(below) Burns plaque on the wall of the Plough Inn, Tarbolton.

Willie's Mill, Tarbolton.

that he had been jilted, Robert sought a change of direction and went off to **Irvine** to learn the trade of flax-dressing. Here he lodged with Alexander Peacock in the Glasgow Vennel; a bronze plaque on the wall commemorates the poet's sojourn here in the winter of 1781-82. In the courtyard of this house stood the heckling-shed where the arduous and unpleasant business of teasing out the flax fibres was carried on and in the loft of which Robert lodged. After a time he obtained better lodgings, renting a small room in a tenement farther down the Vennel for a shilling a week. The **Glasgow Vennel** has been restored by Cunninghame District Council and the heckling-shed now forms part of a museum devoted to Burns and the flax industry. Peacock's house was demolished before 1826 and the site redeveloped; this building now forms the front portion of the museum. House number 4 in the Vennel was traditionally regarded as the place where Robert lodged. This was a two-storey building with a stair on either side of the lobby, the right-hand stair leading to an attic at the back of the house, reputedly the room in which the poet resided. The gallery on the ground floor is used for temporary art exhibitions. The Glasgow Vennel Museum is open all year round and admission is free (tel: 01294 275059).

At 28 Eglinton Street stands **Wellwood**, a red sandstone town house which is now the property of the Irvine Burns Club, founded in 1827. The Club has a formidable collection of Burns manuscripts and a library that includes a copy of the Kilmarnock Edition, as well as a number of fine paintings and a series of murals by Ted and Elizabeth Odling illustrating the time of Burns in Irvine. The building is open to the public on Mondays, Wednesdays, Fridays and Saturdays from 2.30pm to 4.30pm or by appointment (tel: 01294 274511).

The town also boasts two monuments to the poet. A nine-foot bronze statue by James Pittendreigh MacGillivray was commissioned by a wealthy businessman, John Spiers, and erected in 1896 on **Irvine Town Moor** on the northern outskirts of the town, 150m from Maress Road. The pedestal is decorated with four bas-reliefs: a wreathed shield (front), the toil-worn cotter welcomed home by his wife (north), Burns and Highland Mary (west) and the muse of poetry crowning Burns with laurel (east). A bronze reduction of this statue may be seen in the Alloway Village Hall (p. 5).

In the winter of 1781 Burns suffered a bout of severe depression, causing an almost complete physical and mental breakdown, but by the turn of the year he had made a good recovery. In the spring of 1782 he met Richard Brown, a sea captain six years his senior, who had travelled the world. On Sunday afternoons they would stroll out to the Eglinton Woods on the edge of the town and discuss a wide range of topics which must have broadened Robert's mind and stimulated his imagination. To Brown goes the credit of having first put in Robert's head the notion of getting his poems into print, though

The heckling shed, Glasgow Vennel, Irvine, where Burns learned the trade of flax-dressing in 1781.

The Cotter's Saturday Night bas-relief, Burns Statue, Irvine.

he delayed for several years in implementing the suggestion. On the anniversary of Burns's birthday and its own centenary in 1927, the Irvine Burns Club erected a memorial at **St Bryde's Well** (or the Drukken Steps) in Eglinton Woods to mark the occasion which led indirectly to the publication of Burns's poems four and a half years later. In 1976 the cairn was moved about 700m as a result of the development of the Irvine by-pass and is now in **Mackinnon Terrace** on the south-eastern outskirts of the town.

In Mauchline th
six prop

e dwells

young belles

2
MOSSGIEL, 1784–88

Although one of Burns's earliest European biographers, Auguste Angellier (1893) waxed rhapsodic—'Mossgiel, Mossgiel, how that name sings itself into every Scottish heart'—the farm to which the Burnes family moved in the early spring of 1784 was no better than Lochlie in many respects. It was less stony and the soil was lighter, but the drainage was every bit as bad. Robert blamed his own failure as a farmer at Mossgiel on bad seed, but bad luck and a succession of harsh winters and cold, wet summers were more to blame. Despite the popular myth of the absent-minded ploughman, too preoccupied with composing rhyme to plough a straight furrow, Burns was a conscientious and hard-working farmer. The fact that his brother Gilbert fared no better on his own, and had to be extricated from debt by Robert, proves that point. The farm's name should have been a warning, for Mossgiel—or Mossgaville in the older spelling—indicated boggy ground. The light soil, eroded by generations of poor husbandry and the relentless efforts of the weather, lay above thick clay which prevented surface water from running off.

There were, in fact, three farms by this name, known as Near (East), Far (West) and Nether (South) **Mossgiel**. The last named disappeared early in the nineteenth century, but West Mossgiel is a working farm to this day, as is East Mossgiel where the Burns family lived. It was at this time that Robert and Gilbert mutually agreed to alter the spelling of their surname, and the rest of the family fell into line, dropping the 'e'. The farmhouse was substantially rebuilt in 1858-70 when a second storey and a new

Mossgiel Farm, Mauchline.

*Mauchline Castle, home of
Burns's landlord and friend,
Gavin Hamilton.*

roof were added, while the present range of outbuildings bears
no relation to the stable, barn and byre of Burns's day.

In the 1780s the farm belonged to Gavin Hamilton, a lawyer
whose own residence was in the ancient **Castle** of Mauchline,
little more than a mile (1.6 km) to the south. He himself built the
small farmhouse which he originally planned to use as a summer
house. With two rooms on the ground floor and a floored loft
above (used, as at Lochlie, as sleeping accommodation for the
menfolk), Mossgiel was no improvement so far as the Burns
family was concerned. But if disillusionment soon set in
regarding the prospects of the farm, for Robert at least there were
the twin consolations of rhyme and love. Hitherto rather
awkward where the fair sex was concerned, Robert fairly
blossomed after the restrictive influence of his father was
removed. Some controversy surrounds the question whether or
not William Burnes tried to prevent his eldest son from attending
a dancing class at Tarbolton. Robert later confessed to having
defied his father in this matter, though Gilbert tried to play it
down. Be that as it may, 1784 was the year of Robert's sexual
awakening, with dire results, for he impregnated Elizabeth Paton
and he and the unfortunate girl were compelled to do penance

(top) Mauchline Kirk.
(bottom) Cauldon Pottery pot-lid
showing a scene from 'Tam o'
Shanter' c.1860.

in Tarbolton Kirk. Betsey had been employed as a servant at Lochlie but did not move with the family to Mossgiel. She had returned to her parents' home at Largieside, a mile (1.6 km) south of Lochlie, before giving birth to a daughter in 1785. The birth of 'Dear-bought Bess' inspired the tender poem genteelly entitled 'A Poet's Welcome to his Love-begotten Daughter' (but which Burns himself more pithily described as 'Welcome to a Bastart Wean').

In Mossgiel, however, the wellspring of poesy overflowed; 1785 has been aptly described by Donald Low as Burns's *annus mirabilis*, during which many of the finest poems in the Kilmarnock edition were composed, and therefore representing the most productive year of his all too brief career. 'To a Mouse' recalled an actual incident while ploughing in November 1785, while 'To a Mountain Daisy' could equally be pinpointed to an incident on the farm. 'The Cotter's Saturday Night' harked back to a more idyllic time at Lochlie before the litigation began, while the religious satires lampooned ministers and such 'holy beagles' as William Fisher, 'a celebrated ruling elder' of **Mauchline Kirk**. There were new faces to turn Robert's head, as 'The Belles of Mauchline' testified.

In **Mauchline** itself, a bustling little market town situated about the crossroads where the A76 Kilmarnock-Dumfries and A758 Ayr-Muirkirk roads intersect, there was a whole new social scene on his very doorstep. Time has been kind to the core of the village, and many of the buildings associated with Burns's relatively brief residence have survived to this day. Dominating the scene is the parish church, rebuilt in 1827 on the site of the original, but the kirkyard dates from the seventeenth century and contains many graves and their markers pertaining to the people associated in some way or other with the poet. A marker board on the outer wall indicates the location of no fewer than seventeen graves with Burns connections. In one case, at least, the connection is spurious, for Mary Morrison, daughter of

Adjutant Morrison (grave number 3) was a little girl when Burns lived in the district and could not therefore have been the eponymous heroine of the song. Here will be found Clockie Brown of 'The Court of Equity', George Gibson and his wife Agnes—'Poosie Nansie'—and their daughter 'Racer Jess', the poet's landlord and confidant, Gavin Hamilton, the dedicatee of the Kilmarnock *Poems*, and close by, Holy Willie Fisher himself and the Revd William 'Daddy' Auld. There is also the grave containing the remains of four of the children born to Jean Armour, the master-mason's daughter and the poet's favourite among the Mauchline Belles.

The kirkyard is bounded by the main road to Ayr, now known as Loudoun Street and Main Street. Beyond the church is the Loudoun Arms and opposite is the site of the inn run by William Ronald. On the corner of the Cowgate a quaint doggerel plaque marks the site of the Whitefoord Arms and next door is the Armour house. Across the lane and facing the kirkyard is Poosie Nansie's hostelry, little changed (apart from the slate instead of thatched roof) since the night that Burns looked in at a window and beheld the Jolly Beggars. Nearer the Cross there is the Sun Inn, a favourite haunt of Burns and his cronies James Smith and John Richmond. On the far side of the kirkyard there is Gavin Hamilton's house adjacent to the ruined Castle, and Morton's ballroom where Robert and Jean danced together. Up the Back Causeway towards the High Street there are Nance Tinnock's Inn, the house of Dr John Mackenzie, the poet's friend who attended Jean during her two confinements with twins, the houses of the Smiths and the Richmonds, and of course **Burns House** itself.

An affair begun in the autumn of 1785, after a chance encounter on the village bleaching-green, led to pregnancy by March, when Jean was packed off to relatives in Paisley to avoid the prying eyes of the 'houghmagandie pack'. Believing himself to be jilted by the girl to whom he had given a document

Interior of Burns House, Mauchline.

signifying marriage, Burns took up with the Highland lassie known to posterity as Highland Mary (actually born Margaret Campbell, at Dunoon, in 1766). They parted on the second Sunday in May (14 May 1786), the girl returning to Argyll to prepare to join her lover at Greenock that autumn. According to Cromek and much embellished by Cunningham, the lovers exchanged bibles 'over a purling brook'; tradition has identified this incident with the Faile near its junction with the River Ayr, three miles (4.8 km) west of Mauchline at **Failford** on the Ayr road. A red sandstone pillar with a knob on top was erected by the Burns Federation in 1921 near the alleged spot. It should be noted that the so-called custom of exchanging bibles over running water appears to have been a figment of Cromek's fertile imagination; besides, the Faile is too wide and too deep, even in high summer, for such a custom to have been likely even for such an incurable romantic as Burns.

Meanwhile, James Armour fainted on being apprised of his eldest daughter's pregnancy; but he swiftly recovered, and took the 'unlucky paper' to a lawyer in Ayr, Robert Aiken, and fondly imagined that the irregular marriage had been annulled by the simple expedient of cutting out the names of the contracting persons.

On 10 June, Jean confessed, by letter, to the Mauchline Kirk Session that she was pregnant by Robert Burns. Two weeks later, Burns himself appeared before the Session and during July and August made the requisite three appearances before the congregation on the stool of repentence ('the creepy chair' he called it contemptuously) and incredibly received his certificate of bachelorhood at the conclusion! Not surprisingly, Jean applied to the court for a writ to throw her erstwhile lover 'into jail till I find security for an enormous sum... and I am wandering from one friend's house to another'.

In this anxious period there was no time for versifying. Instead, Robert concluded that the only way out of his troubles was to emigrate, and to this end he secured a position as overseer on a slave plantation in Jamaica. He needed to raise £20 for his fare and outfitting and, casting around for some way of raising the money, he decided to give his poems to a wider audience at long last. Hitherto his poems had circulated within the district in manuscript form; but now he took the gamble of having them published at his own expense.

The only printing press in north Ayrshire at this period was operated by John Wilson of the Star Inn Close in **Kilmarnock**. The wooden press itself was cannibalised in the nineteenth century to make a hideous commemorative chair celebrating the centenary of the poet's birth. This monument to Victorian misplaced ingenuity may be seen in the Birthplace Museum at Alloway (p. 2). The Star Inn Close was demolished in the 1970s during the redevelopment of the town centre, but a simple plaque was erected in the Burns Shopping Centre which occupied the site. This was handsomely replaced in September 1995 by a larger-than-life-size statue group of Burns and Wilson, with busts of Apollo and Hermes, unveiled by HRH the Princess Royal in her capacity as President of the International Burns Festival. The bronze group, by Alexander Stoddart, stands atop a circular sandstone pedestal at the town cross. Some 612 copies of the *Poems* were produced by 31 July 1786, for sale at three shillings (15p) in plain blue paper wrappers and sold partly by advance subscription and partly by direct sale. Within weeks, the book was sold out, Burns netting about £54 from the proceeds. He was keen to try a second edition, but the canny printer thought that the first edition would have exhausted the sales potential and demanded cash up front.

Kilmarnock has many associations with the poet, masonic, religious and social. Near the Cross is the **Laigh Kirk**, scene of 'The Ordination', and a few yards away, on the other side of Kilmarnock Water, stood Begbie's Tavern, while Tam Samson's house was beside the road to Mauchline. In the Kay Park stands

(above) Burns Statue, Kilmarnock. (below) The Laigh Kirk, Kilmarnock.

the **Burns Monument**, erected in August 1879 and originally containing a little museum of relics and manuscripts which have now been removed to **Dean Castle** on the outskirts of the town. At the front of the monument stands a marble statue sculpted by W. Grant Stevenson. Due to vandalism in recent years, the refurbished monument has now been surrounded by a high fence and access is not generally permitted. At the corner of London Road and Elmbank Crescent stands the **Dick Institute**, formerly headquarters of the Burns Federation founded in 1885 to unite the Burns clubs and Scottish societies around the world.

In the weeks following the publication of his *Poems*, Robert rode around Ayrshire visiting old friends, making many new ones, and collecting his subscription money. One of the places visited at this time was **New Cumnock** where he stayed at the local inn (now the Castle Hotel) on 18 August. The wife of John Merry, the innkeeper, was Annie, daughter of John Rankine of Adamhill and an old sweetheart of the poet who wrote 'The Rigs of Barley' for her. Tradition avers that Burns wrote the song 'Sweet Afton' at the inn. In 1973 the New Cumnock Burns Club erected a cairn on the bank of the **Afton Water** at the side of the unclassified road to Craigdarroch that runs due south, about two miles (3.2km) from the village. From New Cumnock Burns rode westwards through Dalmellington to Maybole (p. 10) and thence back to Mossgiel by the end of August.

He was still contemplating emigration when he received word on 3 September 1786 that Jean had just given birth to twins, a boy and a girl named Robert and Jean. His voyage to Jamaica had been postponed on 1 September; it was postponed a second time three weeks later, then aborted altogether. A month later,

(top and right) Burns Monument, Kay Park, Kilmarnock. (below) Burns Cairn, Glen Afton, near Cumnock.

Highland Mary died of a 'malignant fever' at Greenock. Controversy rages to this day over the circumstances of this unfortunate girl's death, but whether she died of typhus aggravated by childbirth is still hotly debated. In the nineteenth century the controversy split the Burns Cult into the Mariolaters (who believed that 'Mary' was a 'maiden, pure, divine' who saved Burns from his baser instincts) and the Episodists (who believed that she had been nothing more than a passing fancy, a 'lightskirts' and a kept woman with whom the poet had dallied while Jean Armour was denied to him). Whatever, and despite endless speculation, the girl remains a very shadowy figure.

Although not yet reconciled to Jean Armour, Robert felt that the pressure to leave the country in disgrace was receding. In August and September he had been travelling around the county gathering the subscription money and being gratified by the response to his poems. He finally abandoned his emigration plans when he received, via the Revd George Lawrie of Loudoun, a letter of praise and encouragement from the Revd Dr Thomas Blacklock of Edinburgh, one of the acknowledged *literati* of the time. Visiting the Loudoun manse at **St Margaret's Hill,** at 116 Loudoun Road, Newmilns, in September 1786 Robert was entertained by Christina Lawrie, the first time the poet had heard a harpsichord. That evening the Lawrie family indulged their favourite pastime of dancing, and Robert partnered Lawrie's other daughter, Louisa. From this brief overnight visit came three poems—the prayer 'O Thou Dread Power', 'The Night Was Still' and 'Rusticity's Ungainly Form'. Blacklock's letter induced Robert to try for a second edition in Edinburgh where his poems would reach a far wider public. Meanwhile he was swithering about getting on with farming, a labour he found increasingly repellent, and seeking a new career such as the Excise service.

On 15 November 1786 his long-running correspondence with Mrs Frances Wallace Dunlop of Dunlop began. **Dunlop House,** on the unclassified road between Neilston and Dunlop village, a mile (1.6 km) east of the latter, is no longer extant, the present mansion having been built in 1834. Burns visited Mrs Dunlop there on at least five occasions, and stayed overnight on three of these visits. On 27 November, however, Robert took the most important step in his career; mounted on a borrowed pony, he set off for Edinburgh, travelling by Muirkirk and **Covington** in Lanarkshire, (where a cairn celebrating the bicentenary of his visit was unveiled in 1986), and arriving in the capital on the morning of 29 November.

He had two immediate aims: to secure a second edition of his poems and, if possible, to solicit a well-paid public position. A sinecure in the Salt Office was one possibility, an Army commission was another; even the newly established Chair of Agriculture at Edinburgh University was tentatively considered. In the end, however, he began the long and arduous process of obtaining a commission in the Excise. He would not actually undergo the necessary preliminary training (at Tarbolton) till April 1788, nor receive his commission till 14 July that year, but an actual appointment would not be forthcoming until 1 September 1789.

In the meantime he was lionised by Edinburgh society and acquitted himself well, turning out to be neither the unlettered rustic nor, indeed, the Heav'n-inspired ploughman conjured up by Henry Mackenzie and other fashionable critics. In January 1787 he was hailed as 'Caledonia's Bard' by the gentlemen of the Grand Lodge of Scotland. Undoubtedly Burns did not venture to Edinburgh with the paucity of introductions that he later liked to make out. Influential local masons, in Tarbolton, Mauchline, Kilmarnock and Loudoun, ensured that his arrival in Edinburgh was warmly received. James Dalrymple of Orangefield (1752-95) was first cousin to the powerful Earl of Glencairn, to whom he addressed the letter introducing his friend and fellow mason. Incidentally, Orangefield House at one

Restaurant, Prestwick Airport.

time formed a part of the original terminal buildings at **Prestwick Airport**, where the connections with the poet are evident to this day in the Burns Country Table restaurant and a mural portrait that appropriately decorates the Customs inspection hall.

The Edinburgh period, which spanned almost two years, may be lightly sketched. On 14 December 1786 William Creech issued proposals for the second (first Edinburgh) edition of the *Poems*. A month later Burns met Patrick Miller of Dalswinton and discussed the possible lease of a farm on his estate near Dumfries. Proofreading was well in hand by 22 March and the promised edition appeared on 17 April. A week later Burns sold his copyright to Creech for 100 guineas, though the reluctance of the publisher to settle the account, as well as pay over the money accumulated in royalties and subscription sales, kept Robert hanging about Edinburgh far longer than he had intended. In the interim, he embarked on the first of four tours to various parts of Scotland, undertaken in that hectic year. From 5 May to 1 June he toured the Lothians and the Borders, for part of the time in the company of Robert Ainslie, and crossed northern England from Berwick to Carlisle, and thence to Dumfries where he was made an honorary burgess on 4 June.

Burns was back in Mauchline by 8 June, and now found that his national celebrity had overcome the prejudices of the Armour family. Jean was virtually thrown at him by her parents, with inevitable results, and a pregnancy that would yield a second set of twins the following March. But by the end of June Robert was restless and was off on a second jaunt, this time a trip which took him by Dumbarton and Loch Lomond to Inveraray. Ostensibly he was collecting subscription money due to him, but it seems probable that on the homeward journey he visited the Campbell family, then resident at Greenock–whether he was well received or not is a matter for speculation. This time he hardly paused at

Mauchline to draw breath before he set off for Edinburgh again. On 25 August he began a tour of the Highlands in the company of William Nicol and travelled via Stirling and Blair Atholl as far as Inverness, then round the coast to Buchan and Aberdeen and finally making a sentimental pilgrimage to Kincardineshire and Angus to meet cousins and other relatives. He returned to Edinburgh on 16 September. In October, the last of the four tours was spent in Stirlingshire and Clackmannanshire, tentatively pursuing Peggy Chalmers (who was already secretly engaged to Lewis Hay). Back in Edinburgh on 20 October, he was brought down to earth by the grim news that his daughter Jean had died suddenly.

In November he began serious collaboration with James Johnson on *The Scots Musical Museum* and met Patrick Miller again to discuss the lease of a farm near Dumfries. On 4 December 1787 he met Mrs Agnes McLehose (1758-1841) at a tea party given by Erskine Nimmo and, delayed in Edinburgh by a coach accident which dislocated his knee, he embarked on a torrid courtship of the comely grass widow, mainly by correspondence in which they used the pen-names of Sylvander and Clarinda.

It was not until 18 February 1788 that Burns could tear himself away from Edinburgh and return to Ayrshire. Meanwhile long-suffering Gilbert and his brothers and sisters were having to cope with the rigours of Mossgiel without him. A further five days passed, however, before Robert was reunited with Jean, now almost nine months pregnant. To Ainslie he wrote that he found poor Jean 'banished like a martyr, forlorn, destitute and friendless'. Having secured temporary accommodation for her at Willie's Mill, Tarbolton (p. 12), he rented rooms from the tailor Archibald Meikle on the upper floor of a house in the Back Causeway where twin girls were born on 3 March but died, unnamed and unbaptised, on 10 and 22 March respectively. This building, now known as **Burns House**, was purchased on behalf

Burns House and Museum, Mauchline.

of the Burns Federation in 1915 and is now a museum devoted to Burns as well as the celebrated Mauchline decorative woodware and exhibits on the history of curling. Previously, in June 1902, a marble and bronze plaque was erected on the wall by the Glasgow Rosebery Burns Club. The neighbouring house belonged to Dr John Mackenzie and was purchased by the Federation in 1917 and amalgamated with the museum. Mackenzie's wife Helen was the Miss Miller mentioned in 'The Belles of Mauchline'. The museum is open from Easter till the end of September (tel: 01290 550045).

Meanwhile Burns had been down to Dumfriesshire at the end of February, accompanied by his father's old friend John Tennant of Glenconner, to inspect Ellisland farm. Between the deaths of the two babies, Robert set off for Edinburgh once more on 13 March and signed the lease for Ellisland there five days later. On 20 March he left Edinburgh without succeeding in getting the wily Creech to settle accounts with him. During April and May he was receiving Excise instruction under James Findlay and on or about 10 June he left Mossgiel to take up the lease of his new farm.

It was not until 5 August 1788 that Burns acknowledged his irregular marriage to Jean Armour and paid a guinea to the Kirk Session by way of penance—'the buttock hire' is how he dismissed it. A further four months would elapse before Jean, accompanied by her sole surviving child, little Robert, would be able to make the journey south to join her husband. In November, however, Jenny Clow, the tubercular maidservant of Mrs McLehose, gave birth to a son by him. Though suffering from a wasting disease, Jenny refused to give up her baby. Clarinda was a suitably outraged intermediary in the subsequent negotiations between her erstwhile maid and the unrepentant father.

Mauchline has long since forgiven Burns for his peccadilloes. In the run-up to the centenary of his death the Glasgow

Cottage Homes, Mauchline. (inset) National Burns Monument, Mauchline.

Mauchline Association began raising funds for a **National Burns Memorial and Cottage Homes**. The idea, launched in July 1895, progressed enthusiastically, and by 23 July 1896 the foundation stone was laid with all masonic pomp and ceremony. The memorial, a Gothic extravaganza in red sandstone 67 feet (21m) high, was inaugurated on 7 May 1898 and divided into three floors which for many years housed an odd assortment of relics, ranging from an oil painting of Maria Riddell to cork models of Burns landmarks made by inmates of the Ayrshire Deaf and Dumb Mission. Mercifully much of this has been swept away to make room for a fine audio-visual display on the middle level and an exhibition devoted to the history of coal-mining and the Scottish Labour movement on the upper floor. The tower is open all year round as the local tourist information office and affords magnificent panoramic views of the Burns Country from the roof (tel: 01290 551916).

The cottages, behind the tower and extending along both the minor road to Mossgiel and the main A76 Dumfries-Kilmarnock road, consisted originally of two single and three double apartments, one of the original tenants being the widow of a great-grandson of the bard. Over the years the charity has expanded to provide some twenty cottages whose tenants occupy them rent-free and even receive an annual supplement to their pensions. After the Second World War the Glasgow and District Association of Burns Clubs raised over £15,000 to purchase land from Mossgiel farm and erect ten cottages which were inaugurated on 20 June 1959 as part of the celebrations marking the bicentenary of the birth of Burns. It was singularly appropriate, however, that the new cottages be designated the **Jean Armour Burns Houses**. At last this worthiest of all Burns's heroines has her own memorial, and a most fitting one at that.

How love
thy

3

ELLISLAND, 1788-91

The farm of **Ellisland** extends to some 170 acres (68.9 hectares) and lies on the west bank of the River Nith almost six miles (9km) north of Dumfries. The farm is approached by a narrow road running about 500m east of the A76 Dumfries-Kilmarnock road. Recently, extensive improvements have included good parking facilities for visitors.

Ellisland is in the parish of Dunscore and was part of the ancient barony of Closeburn, lands which belonged to the Comyns but were seized by King Robert Bruce early in the fourteenth century. The estate of Dalswinton on the opposite side of the Nith passed into the hands of the Stewarts and latterly the Maxwells. Dalswinton estate was purchased in 1785 by Patrick Miller (1731-1815) who separately purchased Ellisland for £1300 the following year from James Veitch of Elliock. Miller, a Director of the Bank of Scotland, is best remembered for his experiment with steamboats. In the year that Burns came to Nithsdale, Miller commissioned James Taylor and William Symington to build a twin-hulled boat whose paddles were powered by steam. This vessel made its maiden voyage on Dalswinton Loch on 14 October 1788. A tradition that Burns was a passenger on that historic trip is not confirmed by the poet; a letter to his wife written that very day makes no mention of the occasion.

Both the Dalswinton estate and Ellisland farm in particular were in a rundown state when Miller purchased them, but he made many improvements, introducing the Swedish turnip, a drill plough, an improved threshing machine and the technique of feeding cattle on steamed potatoes.

Burns was given the choice of three farms on the estate, two on the Dalswinton side of the river, on level ground, but opted for Ellisland largely because of its panoramic views. It was, as he later confessed, 'a poet's choice'. Miller gave Burns £300 with which to build a farmhouse and fence the fields. The rent was fixed at £50 per annum for the first three years, rising to £75 for the rest of the 76-year lease. Despite reservations, Robert entered into his lease at Whitsunday (25 May 1788) but did not actually commence work on his farm until 11 June. Two days later he wrote to Mrs Dunlop describing the appalling conditions in which he was now living, 'a solitary Inmate of an old smoky SPENCE; far from every Object I love or by whom I am belov'd...' He lodged in a hut that reeked of damp and peat-smoke and wallowed in homesickness and longing for his Jean.

During the summer of 1788 he travelled regularly back and forth between Ellisland and Mauchline. While Jean and her little son moved into Mossgiel where she was taught the skills of cheese and butter making by old Mrs Burnes and the poet's sisters, Robert was supervising the building of his farmstead and getting in the harvest. The 'hovel in which I shelter' was in fact the humble cottage of the outgoing tenant, David Cullie and his wife Agnes, which stood at the southern end of the farm. Part of the agreement regarding Burns's tenancy was that he was to pay

Ellisland from the south, showing the Spence window.

Original Carron Ironworks range installed by Burns at Ellisland in 1788.

Cullie for the crops harvested at the end of the first season. A receipt for £36 1s 6d in Robert's handwriting, signed by David Cullie, is extant. Two of the four known letters from Burns to Jean date from this period and indicate the progress he was making. In October he wrote to say that he had had the offer of a furnished house nearby over the winter till the farmhouse was ready. This was **The Isle**, bordering Ellisland to the south, which was the summer residence of the Dumfries lawyer, David Newall who offered the accommodation rent-free so long as Robert and Jean kept the house aired.

The second letter shows that Robert originally planned to go to Mauchline on Sunday 19 October to collect Jean and little Bobby, but they continued to live at Mossgiel for several weeks longer. Robert made two further trips to Ayrshire later on, ferrying Jean's goods and chattels, including a splendid four-poster bed, a wedding present from Mrs Dunlop. He was certainly in Mauchline in mid-November, but he set off on his last trip north on 26 November, collected his wife and son, and was back at The Isle with his family by 7 December.

The design and construction of the farmhouse were superintended by Thomas Boyd (1753-1822), a stonemason, building contractor and architect of Dumfries who was also responsible for the New Bridge over the Nith (1791-94) and the Theatre Royal (1792). The actual building was carried out by Alexander Crombie, a stonemason of Dalswinton who also erected cottages in Dalswinton village and worked on Miller's mansion. Burns, as an ardent freemason, performed the laying of the foundation stone of the farmhouse according to the proper masonic rites.

The farmhouse is a single-storey building, but there was access to the loft space which was converted into attics where the domestic and farm servants lodged. In Burns's time the roof was thatched, but in the nineteenth century this was replaced by slates. The ground floor contained five apartments arranged in the form of a letter T. The farmhouse had a parlour on the east, looking down upon the Nith, a west room known as the spence, where distinguished guests would dine with the poet, a kitchen and a bedroom lying between, and a garret. The well from which Jean drew the water lay below the bank beyond the house and close to the river. The kitchen garden was enclosed by a stone wall, at the far corner of which was the privy, still extant. A granary, stackyard, byre and stable were behind the dwellinghouse.

It was commonly believed that the farmhouse, as it stood for most of this century, was the identical cottage built in 1788-89, but this appeared to be disproved by the statement of James Grierson of Dalgoner that Burns's original residence was demolished in 1812 and the farmhouse substantially rebuilt, with a new kitchen and scullery added. A detailed architectural survey carried out in 1993-94, however, revealed that the present building was substantially the house erected in 1788-89, with internal alterations as well as external accretions. During 1995, as part of a programme of refurbishment and renovation, the farmhouse was painstakingly restored to the layout and condition of the 1790s. At the same time the first phase of converting the outbuildings was undertaken to transform Ellisland into a museum that would truly reflect its unique status: the only one of the four farms associated with Burns which has been preserved intact, and the only one which combined all the major facets of his career, as a farmer, Excise officer and poet.

Even before the restoration work of 1995, however, it was possible to capture the atmosphere of Burns at Ellisland. The kitchen ceiling still had the meat-hooks on which Jean smoked her hams, as well as the Carron range and 'swee' which Burns installed for his young bride—the latest in culinary technology two centuries ago. The light and airy parlour, with windows on two sides, was used by Burns as an office and study, and it was here that he would laboriously write up his Excise reports and

The Granary, Ellisland.

accounts, as well as transcribe his poetic compositions. The parlour occupies the southeastern end of the building and from the gable windows one catches beautiful glimpses of the Nith beyond the tree-shaded path where Robert regularly exercised.

Boyd and Crombie were unduly optimistic in promising a date on which the work would be completed. Extant correspondence between Burns and his architect show that the job was still in progress as late as March 1789, though Burns got his revenge by delaying settling the account until April 1791!

Like all of the other farms that Burns worked, Ellisland was situated on poor, unimproved soil. He immediately set to work liming the ground and clearing stones, reorganising the old rigs into straight 15-foot (4.6m) rigs to facilitate drainage through surface run-off. William Clark was hired as ploughman, while Elizabeth Smith was taken on as a farm servant. Burns later switched from arable farming to dairying, leaving Jean and the servants to cope with the milking and making of butter and cheeses, while he concentrated on his Excise duties. Robert kept about ten cows as well as heifers and calfs. For one cow and her calf he got £18—a record price at a time when the average price was £2 10s. To Burns is given the credit for introducing Ayrshire cattle to Nithsdale, and this experiment was carried on with all the enthusiasm and single-mindedness that were the hallmarks of every endeavour he put his mind to. These incontrovertible facts, well attested in contemporary records, rebut the canard that Burns was not cut out to be a farmer. His only mistake was to turn down the infinitely more fertile farms of Bankhead and Foregirth, across the Nith in the parish of Kirkmahoe.

It has also been stated that Burns also kept five horses and several pet sheep. One of the horses was called Pegasus and was Robert's favourite mount. Another horse was a mare belonging to William Nicol and named Peg Nicolson (after a deranged woman who tried to assassinate King George III). Both horses feature in several of Burns's poems.

Robert's early misgivings about his decision were soon confirmed. By the end of July 1789 he was writing to Robert Graham of Fintry, 'deliberating whether I had not better give up farming altogether'. By 11 January 1790 he had had enough: 'This farm has undone my enjoyment of myself', he confessed to his brother Gilbert, 'it is a ruinous affair on all hands. But let it go to hell! I'll fight it out and be off with it'. By now, his career in the Excise promised to be more lucrative and less of a gamble. Since September 1789 he had been employed as a riding officer in the Dumfriesshire Itinerary covering the ten parishes of northern Nithsdale, and entailing riding 200 miles (320 km) every week in all weathers. The die was cast on 27 January 1790 when Robert was placed on the list of officers eligible for promotion to Examiner or Supervisor. The following July he was transferred to the Dumfries Third Division.

Thereafter he was keen to divest himself of what had proved to be a bad bargain. Fortunately, he was allowed to get out of the lease because the farmer of the adjacent property, Laggan, offered Miller £1900 for Ellisland. Miller himself was anxious to get rid of the farm, separated from his other properties by the Nith and accessible only via Auldgirth Bridge three miles (4.8 km) away. In the autumn of 1791 Burns wrote to Peter Hill: 'I have sold to my Landlord the lease of my farm, & as I roup off every thing then, I have a mind to take a week's excursion to see old acquaintances'. The crops were auctioned on 25 August and the farmhouse formally renounced on 10 September, but the Burns family continued to occupy the house till 11 November when they moved to Dumfries.

Ellisland may lack the charisma of the cottage at Alloway where Burns was born, and the sombre memories of the house in Dumfries where he died, but it is nevertheless of surpassing interest to Burns enthusiasts. He was twenty-nine years old, in

(above) Plaque at Ellisland.
(left) 'The carlin claught her by the rump' – a Tam o' Shanter potlid, by the Cauldon Pottery, c.1860.

the prime of life and at the peak of his powers, when he came to Ellisland, full of high hopes and firm resolution. Some of his best poetry was written here, including 'Tam o' Shanter' which local tradition (contradicted by the facts as expressed in the poet's letters) maintains was composed in a single day. The Ellisland period was to see over 130 poems and songs, some of his best nature poems, rousing political ballads and tender love songs as well as experiments in occasional odes and the reworking of old fragments to produce lyrical gems for James Johnson and George Thomson. Some 230 of the 700 extant letters of the poet were written during the Ellisland period, a voluminous output by any standards, and including some of his best polemical writing to the newspapers. Burns also had ambitions to write plays, and sketched out the scenario for a historical drama from the time of King Robert Bruce.

During the Ellisland period Burns was influenced by his close friendship with Robert Riddell of Glenriddell (1755-94) whose estate, **Friars' Carse**, lay to the north of Ellisland. This splendid eighteenth-century mansion is now a hotel boasting 20 fully modernised bedrooms and a dining room which was the venue for the drinking contest celebrated by Burns in 'The Whistle'. Burns was a frequent guest here, even after he left the neighbourhood, until that fateful evening when the drunken frolic known to posterity as 'The Rape of the Sabine Women' led to a breach with the Riddell family. It was for Riddell that Burns prepared the volumes of poems and letters known as the Glenriddell Manuscripts, now in the National Library of Scotland. With Riddell, Burns collaborated in founding and operating the Monkland Friendly Society in **Dunscore**, one of the oldest public libraries in Scotland whose books are preserved at Ellisland to this day. Today, one may stroll the grounds and wooded policies of Friars' Carse and visit the recently restored **Hermitage** at the southern end, close to the boundary with Ellisland. Riddell provided the poet with a key to this little stone summer house and here he wrote a number of poems, including the two versions of 'Verses in Friars' Carse Hermitage'. Other lines, scratched by the poet on window-panes of the Hermitage, have been removed for safe-keeping to the Burns Centre, Dumfries (p. 45). It was at Friars' Carse that Burns met Captain Francis Grose (1731-91), for whose *Antiquities of Scotland* he composed 'Tam o' Shanter'; and it was here also that he was introduced to Riddell's pretty young sister-in-law, the witty and talented Maria Banks Woodley (1772-1808), wife of Walter Riddell who resided at Woodley Park in Troqueer parish in 1792-94. To Maria would fall the lot of compiling a lengthy obituary of Burns for publication in the Dumfries *Standard*, the earliest biography of him.

Another close friend of the Ellisland period was John McMurdo(1743-1803), Chamberlain to the Duke of Queensberry at **Drumlanrig**, and several poems, songs and letters from Burns testify to his close association with the McMurdo family. It was here that Burns met Stephen Clarke (1744-97), the Edinburgh organist and composer with whom he collaborated on many works for Johnson's *Scots Musical Museum*. To McMurdo, Burns lent his collection of bawdy verse, published posthumously under the title of *The Merry Muses of Caledonia*.

The Burns family worshipped regularly in **Dunscore Parish Church**, though Robert had rather a low opinion of the minister, the Revd Joseph Kirkpatrick (1750-1824), and was goaded by his sermon on the centenary of the Glorious Revolution to write a letter to the *Edinburgh Evening Courant* on 8 November 1788 defending the ousted Stuart dynasty. In Sir John Sinclair's *Statistical Account of Scotland*, Kirkpatrick's account of Dunscore parish has an appendix by Burns giving a report on the Monkland Friendly Society.

John Morrin of Laggan sold Ellisland farm to James Taylor of Netherholm in 1805 for £4430. It remained in the Taylor family till 1921 and latterly the daughter of the tenant had acted as

Dunscore Parish Kirk.

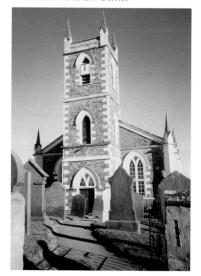

unofficial curator, showing interested Burnsians over the poet's parlour. In 1921 the farm was bought by George Williamson for £3450 with the aim of preserving it in memory of Burns. A trust was subsequently established and Ellisland bequeathed in October 1922 to 'the Sheriff Principal of the County of Dumfries, the Sheriff Substitute of said County, the Provost of the Burgh of Dumfries' and others as trustees. On the death of John Williamson (brother of the late George) in 1928 the trust came into effect. While the fields have continued to be worked by a series of tenants, a bungalow being erected nearby for the use of a farmworker, the farmhouse itself was preserved as a museum of relics and manuscripts, but it is only now (1996) that this has been organised on a proper commercial footing.

Various plaques were erected by the trustees on fences and gates around the property, but to celebrate the bicentenary of the poet's arrival a plaque by the doorway of the farmhouse was unveiled by Sheriff-Principal Gillies in June 1988. Burns's career as a farmer was highlighted by a permanent exhibition inaugurated on 25 October 1979 by Sam Gaw, President of the Burns Federation. The farm's original granary was converted by the trustees to house the display devoted to the seasonal round of farming in the late eighteenth century. More recently, the curator, James Irving, has assembled farming implements and machinery which it is hoped will form the nucleus of further agricultural exhibits.

The displays in Ellisland have been thoroughly overhauled and expanded to illustrate the many facets of Burns's career in this period, not only as a farmer, Exciseman and poet, but as a song collector and folklorist with serious interests in music and drama. In particular, the central role of 'Tam o' Shanter' will be highlighted, as well as 'Auld Lang Syne', composed at Ellisland in December 1788 and now the world's most widely sung song.

The grounds have been landscaped, the walk along the riverbank improved, and a footpath to the Hermitage clearly marked.

4
DUMFRIES, 1791-96

I n November 1791 the Burns family moved into the town of Dumfries, renting three rooms on the upper floor of a house in the Wee Vennel, now **11 Bank Street**, from Captain Hamilton of Allershaw. A plaque marks the spot, but in the 1970s the late James Urquhart added a painted signboard signifying that the building should be regarded as the Song House of Scotland, on account of the many fine lyrics composed by Burns while living there. *The house is in private occupancy and is not open to the public.*

The Burns family then consisted of Robert and Jean with their three sons Robert junior, Francis Wallace (born August 1789), and William Nicol (born April 1791) and Robert's illegitimate daughter Elizabeth whom he had fathered on Ann Park, the barmaid at the **Globe Inn** and second cousin of William Hyslop the publican. During the Dumfries period this was the poet's 'favourite howff', but while he continued to reside at Ellisland he often stayed overnight at the inn if detained in town late on official business. The bedroom on the upper floor, complete with four-poster bed, is preserved as Burns's bedroom, and is decorated with a number of relics, including an oil painting, supposedly a portrait of Burns by Raeburn but probably not Burns and definitely not by the celebrated artist. Downstairs, there is the Burns Room, a small dining room containing the poet's chair and cabinets of Burnsiana. The bar and main dining room are replete with prints, engravings and memorabilia. Externally, little has changed since the Globe was erected in 1610. In Burns's day it belonged to the Hyslop family of Lochend but more recently was purchased by the McKerrow family, prominent in the Burns world. In the courtyard stands a

(opposite) Burns House, Dumfries.
(below) The Globe Inn, Dumfries.

large boulder of Locharbriggs red sandstone bearing the opening lines of 'Ae Fond Kiss', a song written by Burns for Clarinda in December 1791 just after the move to Dumfries. The stone was part of the Dumfries exhibit at the Glasgow Garden Festival in 1988.

In 1792 Burns was promoted to the Dumfries Port Division. His salary now stood at £70 per annum, with a further £20 in perquisites. On 29 February he led one of the squads of Excisemen and dragoons that waded out into the chill waters of the Solway near Gretna and captured the Manx smuggling brig *Rosamond*. Tradition maintains that the song 'The Deil's Awa wi th'Exciseman' was written shortly after this incident, in the upper room of a building in **Annan**, now the Café Royal in the High Street; a sandstone plaque below the clock on the corner of the building records the occasion. The *Rosamond* was towed to the boat-slip at **Kelton** in the Nith estuary for repair, and then disposed by auction on 19 April at **Kingholm Quay** where Robert, in a quixotic gesture, purchased the ship's four carronades and sent them to Paris as a gift to the revolutionary Convention.

Less contentious was Robert's role in promoting the **Theatre Royal** in Shakespeare Street which opened on 29 September 1792. Previously, companies of strolling players had used the Old Assembly Rooms at the foot of the George Inn Close, but Robert Riddell was the prime mover of the Theatre, putting up much of the cash for the project. Burns was intimately connected with the scheme, bringing Alexander Nasmyth from Edinburgh to paint the backdrops and writing soliloquies and addresses for actors and actresses on their benefit nights. A bronze portrait plaque on the wall was erected in October 1960 when the theatre, after many years as a cinema, was purchased by the Guild of Players and restored to its original function. On the night of 28 October 1792 there was a disturbance in the audience, one faction (the Loyal Natives) calling for the national anthem in the

(top) Burns Stone, in courtyard of the Globe Inn.
(above) Tam o' Shanter and Souter Johnie at the fireplace of the Burns Room in the Globe Inn, Dumfries.

Theatre Royal, Dumfries.

middle of a play, and another calling for *Ça Ira*, the anthem of the French Revolution. Burns remained seated but was afterwards denounced to the Excise Board for 'disaffection' and closely questioned on his actions. As a 'humble placeman' he often had to curb his tongue, though his radical views were well known.

The outbreak of war with France in 1793 severely curtailed imports and thus cut Excise perquisites drastically. On 19 May, however, things still looked bright enough for the Burns family, now increased by daughter Elizabeth Riddell (born on 21 November 1792), to move to a much larger house in Millbrae Vennel, now 24 Burns Street. This red sandstone building, known as **Burns House**, was the poet's last residence and his widow continued to reside there until her death in 1834. This

(right) Burns House, Dumfries
(below) Burns's writing desk,
Burns House, Dumfries.

house, too, was rented from Hamilton of Allershaw but in 1851 it was purchased by Colonel William Nicol Burns, and on 25 January 1935 it was formally opened as a museum by Miss Jean Armour Burns Brown, great-granddaughter of the poet. It contains Robert's study and the bedroom in which he died in July 1796 as well as important relics and Burnsiana. It is open all year round with seasonal and time variations (tel: 01387 255297).

More than anywhere else, Dumfries has the stamp of Burns upon it. Everywhere, there are signs and markers as well as plaques alluding to some Burns connection. Near Burns House is **St Michael's Church** where the Burns family worshipped. The original box pew has long since vanished but a brass marker inset in one of the pillars indicates the location. More recently, windows commemorating Burns and Jean were erected on the initiative of the Burns Howff Club to celebrate its centenary in 1989.

In **St Michael's Kirkyard** there is a stone pedestal south of the church which bears a diagrammatic plate showing the location of 45 graves of people associated with the poet, ranging in relevance from the banker James Gracie and the Hyslops of the Globe Inn to Dr Archibald Blacklock whose sole connection was that he examined the skull of Burns in 1834 when the vault was opened for the interment of Jean Armour. The town's most prominent landmark, the **Mid Steeple,** is immortalised in lines of Burns's patriotic song 'Does Haughty Gaul Invasion Threat?' when the poet became a founder member of the Royal Dumfries Volunteers and drilled with other members of 'the awkward squad' in the **Dock Park**, where a couple of carronades from the French Revolutionary Wars are still to be seen. The Mid Steeple has, below the outside staircase, a plaque by Tim Jeffs erected in 1959 to mark the bicentenary of the poet's birth and showing a relief map of the burgh in the time of Burns. At the other end of the High Street, opposite Greyfriars' Church, stands **Burns Statue**, in Italian marble, with quotations from three of

Burns's best-loved poems engraved on the plinth. Sculpted by Amelia Hill, it was unveiled by the Earl of Rosebery on 6 April 1882.

Relics of the poet were once displayed in the **Burgh Museum**, formerly an observatory and, before that, a windmill on Corbelly Hill, Terregles Road, overlooking the town from the west bank of the Nith. In 1986, however, many relics and manuscripts were transferred to the **Robert Burns Centre**, formally opened by HRH Princess Alexandra. The Centre was previously the Town Mill, erected in 1781, and includes an audio-visual theatre illustrating the poet's life in the town, exhibition areas, a cafeteria (Jean Armour's Pantry) and a very well-stocked bookshop. The displays include a seated figure of Burns the Exciseman, the Spode punch-bowl and matching crockery purchased by the Dumfries Burns Club at its inauguration in 1820, and a model of the Dalswinton steamboat of 1788. In the entrance hall is the Octocentenary Collage, a tapestry woven in 1986 to mark the 800th anniversary of the royal burgh, though seven of its eight panels actually allude to the town's most celebrated resident. The Centre is open daily,

Burns Centre, Dumfries.

from 10am to 8pm, Monday to Saturday, and from 10am to 5pm on Sundays, April to September; in the winter months from October to March it is open from Tuesday to Saturday, 10am to 1pm and 2pm to 5pm. Admission is free, but there is a small charge for the audio-visual theatre (tel: 01387 264808). Dumfries also boasts a **Burns Garden**, adjoining St Michael's Kirkyard, planted with all the flowers, trees and shrubs referred to in the works of Burns.

Farther afield there is the picturesque **Burns Walk** along the winding Nith, a favourite haunt of the bard, leading to fine vistas of **Lincluden Abbey** across the river in Terregles parish, and immortalised in several of Burns's songs, notably the two versions of 'Ca' the Yowes', 'Grim Grizzel' and 'As I Stood by Yon Roofless Tower'.

In the summers of 1793 and 1794 Burns made two short vacation trips through Galloway in the company of his friend John Syme. On both occasions a number of poems, songs and barbed epigrams resulted. At **Kirkcudbright** the Selkirk Arms Hotel contains an interesting carved wooden plaque by Tim Jeffs with a portrait of Burns and the words of the Selkirk Grace. Contrary to the statement on the sign outside the hotel, however, Burns did not write this grace in the Selkirk Arms in 1794; he recited it at **St Mary's Isle**, home of the Earl of Selkirk, on 1 August 1793, when he was asked to say grace and thereupon gave an extempore rendering of the four lines which have ever afterwards been known as the Selkirk Grace.

Burns and Syme were in **Gatehouse of Fleet** when they beheld the sorry spectacle of the radical lawyer Thomas Muir being led through the village in chains, *en route* to stand trial in Edinburgh on trumped up charges of sedition which resulted in a sentence of transportation to Botany Bay for fourteen years. Out of this incident came 'Scots Wha Hae', long regarded as the Scottish national anthem, which, recalling Bruce's address to his troops before the battle of Bannockburn in 1314, was inspired by

Road sign, Kirkcudbright.

'some other struggles of the same nature, *not quite so ancient*' as Burns reported elliptically to George Thomson when sending him the song.

Portpatrick's connection with the poet is only indirect; it was referred to in one of his letters and was also the town whither Burns's close friend and Excise colleague John Gillespie was posted. But it boasts a curiously emaciated statue of Burns, sculpted by James Watt of Stranraer and erected behind the bowling green in May 1929. In 1983 it was swept away by a landslide in a storm, but was subsequently repaired and re-erected by the Burns Howff Club of Dumfries.

Sanquhar, mid-way between Dumfries and Mauchline, was a frequent stopping place of Burns who stayed overnight at the Queensberry Arms in the High Street kept by his friend Edward Whigham. When, in January 1789, Robert was turned out to make way for the funeral cortège of Mary Oswald of Auchencruive, and forced to ride a further twelve miles (19.2 km), on a cold winter's night, to the inn at New Cumnock (p. 23), he retaliated by penning the vitriolic 'Ode Sacred to the Memory of Mrs Oswald' which brought him a rebuke from Mrs Dunlop: 'Are you not a sad wicked creature to send a poor old wife straight to the Devil, because she gave you a ride in a cold night?' The inn keeps alive the memory of the poet in the Shanter Lounge, with the obligatory heads of Tam and Souter Johnie stuck on the exterior wall. At the head of the High Street is the Tolbooth which now contains the local museum, including relics and memorabilia of the poet who dubbed the burgh 'Black Joan' in his electioneering ballad 'The Five Carlins'.

Burns was also a frequent visitor to **Moffat**, especially on journeys to and from Edinburgh, and stayed at the **Black Bull Inn** founded in 1568. It was here that he composed his epigram on Miss Davies, famed for her petite beauty, wit and charm. A plaque on the wall quotes the lines. Nearby is **Craigieburn**, home of Jean Lorimer, the Chloris of many of Burns's love songs.

The Black Bull Inn, Moffat.

The last years in Dumfries are far from the dissipation and decline so bleakly painted by nineteenth century biographers. In the Excise service Burns made rapid strides, producing a plan for the reorganisation of the Dumfries divisions in 1794 and acting as Supervisor between December 1794 and April 1795. In January 1795 he joined the Volunteers and played an active part in the management of the Corps right up until his last illness. But troubles were looming. His income dropped by a third as the strictures of the war with France grew tighter, and the stress of making ends meet was compounded by personal tragedy. In September 1795 his three-year-old daughter Elizabeth Riddell (named after Robert Riddell's wife) died suddenly and the grieving father was prostrated. That winter he was ill with 'a most severe Rheumatic fever'. By 31 January 1796 he was 'beginning to crawl across my room', but the ensuing three months were marred by the famine in Dumfries and the ugly Meal Riots that resulted.

Burns continued to perform his Excise duties till early June, but the deterioration in his health is graphically reflected in his signature on receipts for his salary. On the advice of his friend and doctor, William Maxwell (1760-1834), Robert went to **Brow on Solway** in Ruthwell parish on 3 July to try to recover his strength. He was ordered to drink the chalybeate water of the **Brow Well**, a spring debouching into a stone tank fitted with an iron drinking-cup. At one time a plaque recording Burns's poignant visit was affixed to the adjoining fence. A few yards away is the Solway Firth with its quicksands and dangerous currents. Here, up to his armpits in water that remains ice-cold all year round, the dying poet endured daily bathing. A ceremony is held at the Brow each July to commemorate the poet. Not surprisingly, he returned to Dumfries on 16 July in poorer shape than before, and took to his bed where he died only five days later. On 25 July 1796 the funeral of Robert Burns, attended not only by the Volunteers but also the two regiments then quartered in the town, as well as thousands of people from the town and surrounding countryside, took place as Jean went into labour and gave birth to a son Maxwell, named after the doctor who had unwittingly hastened the poet's death.

Burns was laid to rest in St Michael's Kirkyard in a plot which he had purchased some time previously. Following the removal of Robert's remains to the **Mausoleum** on the night of 19 September 1817, the vacated lair was given by Jean to her friend Mrs Perochon, the daughter of Mrs Dunlop of Dunlop. In more

Burns Mausoleum, St Michael's Kirkyard, Dumfries.

recent years a simple marker inscribed 'Site of Original Grave of Robert Burns' was affixed to the railings.

The idea of giving Burns a more fitting resting-place was first mooted in November 1813 by John Syme and William Grierson and rapidly grew into an international appeal, raising funds throughout the British Isles, India, America and the colonies. About fifty designs for a memorial were submitted by architects and on 25 April 1815 the plans of Thomas Hunt of London were approved. The actual work was carried out by John Milligan of Dumfries, and the foundation stone laid on 5 June 1815. Peter Turnerelli was selected to sculpt the full-sized marble figures of the muse Coila casting her mantle over Burns at the plough. The last portion of the money required for the project was raised at a great public dinner in London on 25 May 1816. The Mausoleum was built in the style of a Grecian temple, complete with dome and pillared portico, more in character with the sunny Mediterranean than the rich red sandstone of the surrounding tombs and the softer climate of Dumfries, but the effect is

The Muse of Poetry and Burns at the Plough, in the Burns Mausoleum, Dumfries.

dramatic. Unfortunately, the marble did not stand up well to atmospheric pollution and by 1910 the figures were in decay. Plans to restore and renovate the tomb were delayed by the First World War and it was not until 1936 that the damage could be rectified. By that time the original Turnerelli sculpture was beyond repair, so Hermon Cawthra was commissioned to redo the figure group, avoiding Turnerelli's errors in the poet's garb and the details of the plough. Turnerelli's figure of the poet was for some years displayed in Burns House but was subsequently withdrawn and ended up in a builder's yard whence it has long since vanished without trace. The Mausoleum contains the original sandstone slab covering the grave, complete with error in the poet's age at death. Within the vault below are interred the children of Burns who predeceased him, as well as Maxwell (1796-99), Francis Wallace (1789-1803), Jean Armour Burns (1767-1834) and Robert junior (1786-1857). Two marble tablets adorn the walls and record the deaths of James Glencairn (1794–1865) and his family, and William Nicol (1791-1872) and his family. The remains of James Glencairn and William Nicol (who both died in Cheltenham) were interred in the vault beneath their respective tablets. James McClure, a faithful friend of the poet who attended him on his deathbed, died in November 1813 and by permission of the Burns family was interred in the precinct of the Mausoleum, along with his wife Jean Heughan who died in September 1815.

Robert Burns

INDEX OF PLACES